Hearts of Gold

Four True Life Stories About
COMPASSION

COVER ILLUSTRATION:

Justin Ray Thompson

PHOTO CREDITS:

AP/Wide World—Leslie Close/*Daily Progress*, p. 12; Alejandro Ruiz,
p. 14; Ed Bailey, p. 16; Tom Hanson, p. 18; Henrik Laurvik, p. 28
Free the Children—end pages (Craig Kielburger), pp. 20-21, 22
Gamma-Liaison—François Lochon, p. 24; J. C. Francolon, end pages
(Mother Teresa) & pp. 26-27
Give Kids the World—pp. 6, 9, 10

In loving memory of
Jennifer Christine Moser

Copyright © 2002
Kidsbooks, Inc.
230 Fifth Avenue
New York, NY 10001

Visit us at *www.kidsbooks.com*

VALUES IN ACTION ™

Hearts of Gold

Four True Life Stories About

COMPASSION

Compassion is a sympathetic awareness of other people's trouble or pain, and a desire to help ease it. In this book, you will meet four extraordinary people with hearts of gold. Their compassion has helped make life better for countless others.

Henri Landwirth
by Denise Rinaldo

Rigoberta Menchú
by Susan E. Edgar

Craig Kielburger
by Denise Rinaldo

Mother Teresa
by Denise Rinaldo

Henri Landwirth

born 1927

A six-year-old girl named Amy was dying of cancer. Her greatest wish was to visit Walt Disney World and meet Mickey Mouse. Henri Landwirth, a wealthy hotel owner in Orlando, Florida, agreed to provide a hotel room for her and her family. However, Amy died before the trip's details could be ironed out. Upset by her death, Henri vowed to help other seriously ill children achieve their dreams. Using his own money as well as donations, he created Give Kids the World, an organization dedicated to granting sick children's wishes to see Orlando's child-friendly attractions. Today, Give Kids the World is a 51-acre resort that hosts 7,000 sick children and their families each year.

Surviving His Childhood

Henri Landwirth knows how it feels to be a child awaiting death. Born in Antwerp, Belgium, on March 7, 1927, he moved to Poland with his family when he was 3. By the time Henri turned 12, Adolf Hitler had gained power in Germany and had invaded Poland. Hitler's plan was to take over Europe and, at the same time, wipe out the continent's Jewish population. Henri and his family, who were Jewish, were in grave danger.

Soon after the invasion, Henri's father was arrested and imprisoned by the Nazis. Less than a year later, Henri and his twin sister, Margot, were forced onto cattle cars and shipped to a concentration camp.

For five years, Henri was forced to move from one camp to another. Every day, he came face to face with death. People around him suffered or died from starvation, illness, or other inhuman conditions in the camps. Henri himself was hungry all the time, sometimes living for days at a time with only a crust of bread to eat.

He escaped death many times. The last time was in late 1944, when soldiers at one of the camps decided to let him live. "Line up over there facing the trees. I'm not going to shoot you," one soldier told Henri and two other Jewish prisoners. "When I raise my gun, run into the woods."

Henri ran. Near starvation, he wandered alone through the woods for several hundred miles. Finally, he crawled into an empty house and collapsed. He awoke to find a kind old woman standing over him. She told him that the war had ended three days before, and that he didn't need to run anymore.

Henri knew that his father had died early in the war. Henri was crushed when he learned that his mother had died just weeks before the war ended, but overjoyed to find that Margot had survived.

Making Life Better

In 1947, Henri moved to the United States to try to start a new life. He arrived in the country with only $20 in his pocket. He had no education and he couldn't speak English. That didn't stop Henri. After serving in the U.S. Army, he got a job at a New York City hotel and found that he liked the business.

He and his wife, Josephine, moved to Florida in 1954. Soon Henri and Josephine had three children—Gary, Greg, and Lisa—and Henri was managing the Starlight Motel in Cocoa Beach. Nearby, the home of the U.S. space program, called Cape Canaveral, was being built. Henri's motel became a second home for the original Mercury astronauts, all of whom became close friends with Henri. Henri also developed a strong friendship with Walter Cronkite, a legendary TV newsman, who was often in Cocoa Beach reporting on the space program. Later, all these friends helped Henri build Give Kids the World.

Henri became more and more successful in the hotel business. Just as Walt Disney World was getting under way, he bought Holiday Inn franchises in Orlando. All the while, he was involved in charity work, mostly to benefit children and senior citizens. In 1970, he and the Mercury astronauts founded the Mercury Seven Foundation to give science scholarships to students. He also built a senior citizens' home and a clinic for children with cerebral palsy. Still, he wanted

> *"We make a living by what we get, but we make a life by what we give."*
> —Sir Winston Churchill
> (Henri Landwirth's favorite quotation)

Henri Landwirth with children enjoying a Give Kids the World vacation

The Holocaust

Adolf Hitler rose to power in Germany in 1933. He set out to conquer Europe and rid it of anyone he considered alien. He had a special hatred for Jews.

Hitler's Nazi Party began by taking away the rights of Jews in Germany: the rights to vote, own property, and meet with one another. Jews were forced into crowded areas called ghettos. Then, when World War II broke out in 1939, Nazis began to ship Jews to concentration camps. Other Jews were sent to labor camps, where they were forced to work under harsh conditions.

World War II ended with Japan's surrender in 1945. By that time, six million Jews—two thirds of Europe's Jewish population—had been killed. Two of them were Henri Landwirth's parents.

to do more. That led him to found Give Kids the World in 1986.

Many groups throughout the world grant the wishes of dying and seriously ill children. The most common wish by far is a trip to Walt Disney World. All a wish-granting group has to do is call Give Kids the World. Everything is taken care of: the room; tickets for the entire family to Walt Disney World, Sea World, Universal Studios, and other area attractions; the use of a video camera; and free long-distance

phone calls. The resort itself has swimming pools, a water playground, a nature trail, an ice-cream parlor, a theater, and more.

In its first year of operation, Give Kids the World gave trips to 329 children. Today, it runs a 51-acre resort that serves 7,000 families per year. Henri is no longer active in managing his hotels. He spends all of his time working with Give Kids the World. Henri Landwirth survived a childhood of brutality and horror to become one of the most compassionate men in America. "From the desperation of my own childhood," he says, "grew the empathy to serve children facing their own desperate circumstances."

Life Lines

1927 Henri Landwirth and his twin sister are born in Antwerp, Belgium, on March 7. In 1930, the family moves to Poland.

1939-1940 German troops invade Poland. Henri, his mother, and sister are sent to concentration camps.

1945 Soon after Henri escapes from the camp, World War II ends.

1947 Henri moves to the United States. Eventually, he becomes successful in the hotel business.

1970 Henri and NASA's Mercury astronauts found a scholarship program for science students.

1986 Amy, a six-year-old girl with cancer, dies before fulfilling her wish of visiting Walt Disney World. In response, Henri establishes Give Kids the World.

1994 *Parents* magazine names Henri humanitarian of the year.

Rigoberta Menchú

born 1959

Amid the war-torn countryside of Guatemala, a young woman dreamed of a better life for herself and her people—a life in which all people were treated fairly regardless of the color of their skin, their ethnic background, or how much money they had. Instead of sitting idly by, that young woman—Rigoberta Menchú *(men-CHOO)*—turned her dream into action. Her compassion for her fellow people and her belief in fair and equal treatment for all people led her to become one of the leaders in the fight for human rights, native Indian rights, and social justice throughout the world.

Growing Up in Guatemala

Rigoberta Menchú was born on January 9, 1959, in the village of Chimel, in the northern province of El Quiché *(kee-CHAY)*, Guatemala. El Quiché was named for the Quiché, a branch of Mayan Indians who have lived in that region for centuries. The Quiché, who live off the land, are very respectful of nature. Rigoberta's family were Quiché Maya.

When Rigoberta was a young girl, she moved with her family to the west coast of Guatemala. There, they went to work on big *fincas*—the plantations of wealthy landowners. As Rigoberta and her family helped harvest the crops, picking coffee beans and cotton, she began to notice how badly her family was treated by the *finca* owners. For example, when her younger brother died, the family members attended the funeral.

Rigoberta Menchú, visiting with Tzotzil Indians in Mexico. She was serving as an official observer of local elections, helping to ensure that they were conducted fairly.

Since they did not report to work that day, the *finca* owner fired them all. He didn't even pay them for the work they had done earlier that week. Rigoberta believed that this type of treatment was unjust. She grew determined to make things better for her people.

Tragedy for Rigoberta

Like the Menchús, many Guatemalans faced unfair treatment for years. From 1960 to 1996, the country was engaged in a civil war. When Rigoberta was a baby, radical military forces overthrew Guatemala's government. The new leaders waged a ferocious campaign against the indigenous peoples (native inhabitants). As many as 200,000 people disappeared or died in the 36-year struggle. Many

14

Guatemalan citizens, including the native Indians, fought back by raiding military sites and tried to force the military leaders out of power.

By the time Rigoberta was in her late teens, some military officers believed that her family was part of the group fighting against them. This suspicion led to her father, mother, and brother being arrested and eventually killed. Rigoberta says that she never took part in the violence, but she did join several groups that opposed Guatemala's military leadership. Helping one of the groups, she taught peasants how to resist the cruel actions of the military. Later, she led peaceful protests calling for better working conditions on farms and plantations.

Peace for the People

After the deaths of Rigoberta's parents and brother, she received threats against her own life. For safety, she fled to Mexico in 1981. While there, she told the world of the plight of the Indian peoples of Guatemala and spoke out against the suffering there. In 1982, she started an organization called the United Representation of the Guatemalan Opposition (RUOG), aimed at uniting people against the harsh military government.

Nobel Peace Prize

Only nine women have won the Nobel Peace Prize since its inception in 1893. Rigoberta Menchú is one of the nine.

Rigoberta was given that great honor for her continued efforts toward bringing peace to her native country of Guatemala, along with seeking social justice and equality for the indigenous peoples of the Americas and throughout the world.

When presenting her with the Nobel Peace Prize in 1992, the announcer said, "Today, Rigoberta Menchú stands as a vivid symbol of peace and reconciliation across ethnic, cultural, and social dividing lines in her own country, on the American continent, and in the world."

> *"What I treasure most in life is being able to dream. During my most difficult moments and complex situations, I have been able to dream of a more beautiful future."*
> —Rigoberta Menchú

The following year, Rigoberta's story was told in *I, Rigoberta Menchú: An Indian Woman in Guatemala*, a book written by Elisabeth Burgos-Debray, an anthropologist from Venezuela. Burgos-Debray wrote down the story, as told to her by Rigoberta, of the struggles of Rigoberta and her people. *I, Rigoberta Menchú* was so popular that it was translated into 20 languages and has been read the world over.

Rigoberta kept working, driven by her determination to help bring peace and justice to the Guatemalan people. Her compassion and hard work were honored in 1992, when she was awarded the prestigious

People of peace: Rigoberta Menchú, winner of the 1992 Nobel Peace Prize, meets with Kofi Annan, Secretary-General of the United Nations, who won the prize in 2001.

Nobel Peace Prize. The granters of the prize praised her for not turning to violence in times of great struggle and despair in her native country and for choosing, instead, to make a difference through political and social channels. Rigoberta used the $1.2 million in prize money to establish the Rigoberta Menchú Foundation, to help all indigenous peoples. It also has helped Guatemalans who had fled from the country, as Rigoberta had done, to return to their homeland.

In 1993, during the International Year of the Indigenous Peoples, the United Nations named Rigoberta Menchú its Goodwill Ambassador. Today, she remains active in her quest for human and social rights.

Life Lines

1959 Rigoberta Menchú is born in Chimel, Guatemala, on January 9.

1960 Civil war breaks out in Guatemala.

1979 Rigoberta joins the Committee of the Peasant Union, a group formed to support the rights of poor farm workers.

1981 Rigoberta flees to Mexico to escape from death threats.

1983 *I, Rigoberta Menchú* is published.

1992 Rigoberta is awarded the Nobel Peace Prize.

1993 Rigoberta is named Goodwill Ambassador by the UN.

1996 Guatemala's government signs a peace treaty, ending the country's 36-year-long civil war.

PRESS GALLERY

Craig Kielburger

born 1982

One morning in April 1995, 12-year-old Craig Kielburger read a newspaper article that changed his life. It was about the death of another 12-year-old boy, Iqbal Masih of Pakistan. Iqbal had been a child laborer, sold into slavery by his parents when he was only four years old. For six years, Iqbal was chained to a loom and forced to weave carpets. At age 10, he escaped and became an international crusader against child labor. Then, Iqbal was murdered—perhaps by carpet makers who wanted to silence him. When Craig learned Iqbal's story, he vowed to do something to help. That week at school, Craig founded a group called Free the Children. Since then, Free the Children has exploded into an international movement of kids helping kids, with 150,000 members and chapters in 20 countries.

A Need to Help Others

Craig Kielburger was born December 17, 1982, in Toronto, Canada. Even as a little boy, Craig had compassion for the less fortunate, and an urge to help people. "If he saw a child alone on the playground, he'd be the one to go up to him," Craig's mother has said.

When Craig first read about Iqbal Masih, his heart broke. He wanted to help, but realized that he would first have to become more informed. So Craig did some research. He learned that, worldwide, more than 250 million children were forced to weave carpets, make fireworks, pick crops, and perform other difficult jobs. Many, like Iqbal, were practically slaves. With that knowledge, Craig took action. He asked his seventh-grade teacher if he could talk to the class about child labor. The teacher said yes. A little nervous, Craig stood before his classmates and told them about the situation. He said that kids lucky enough to live in freedom should band together to help children forced into labor. "Who will join me?" he asked. Immediately, 18 kids raised their hands. That was the beginning of Free the Children (FTC).

Craig Kielburger (top right) *with other Free the Children members*

From an office at Craig's house, FTC members began writing to government leaders and circulating petitions pressuring companies not to use child labor in their factories. Their first victory was getting the city of Toronto to ban the use of child-made fireworks in city celebrations. (Their research had uncovered the fact that 12 working children had recently been killed in an explosion in a fireworks factory in India.)

As word spread about FTC, more and more kids joined. The group's big breakthrough came in the fall of 1995, when Craig was asked to speak to a convention of the Ontario Federation of Labor. When Craig finished his speech, the audience stood and cheered. One union's representative ran to the stage and pledged $5,000 for Free the Children. Then another did the same. By the time Craig left, $150,000 had been

pledged. With the money, FTC helped build an education center in Alwar, India, for children freed from slavery as carpet workers.

When the next school year started, a young human-rights activist invited Craig to accompany him to South Asia to witness child labor first-hand. At first, Craig's parents refused to let him go. The trip would be too dangerous, they thought, and Craig was too young. But Craig persuaded them to change their minds.

In December 1995, he boarded a plane headed for Dhaka, Bangladesh, a city in southern Asia. Traveling though Bangladesh, India, Nepal, Thailand, and Pakistan, he saw terrible poverty. He talked with children who worked as carpet weavers, household servants, and brick makers. He met Iqbal's mother and had an audience with Mother Teresa.

As a result of Craig's trip, many news organizations—including the TV news program *60 Minutes*—did stories about Craig and FTC. With the publicity, donations came flooding in, and children all over the world began forming FTC chapters of their own.

"Kids can make a difference. Knowledge is the key, knowledge is the power. Take that power and bring about change."
—Craig Kielburger

Taking a Stand

Craig offers this advice to kids who want change the world for the better.

Choose a cause.
The world is filled with worthy causes: child labor, world hunger, animal welfare, and many others. Pick the one closest to your heart.

Educate yourself.
Using the library, the Internet, teachers, and your parents, learn all you can about your chosen cause. Start an information file.

Build a team.
Find other kids who want to help you. Form a group and decide on a name.

Set goals and a plan.
List your goals, then draw up a plan for reaching each one. You might launch a letter-writing campaign, hold a demonstration, or circulate a petition.

Keep trying.
If your group doesn't take off at first, don't give up. Try a different approach. As Craig often quotes, "A journey of a thousand miles starts with one step."

Going Forward

FTC has built 200 schools in developing countries, set up medical clinics in Nicaragua, and built a rescue home in India for children who had been forced to smuggle illegal drugs. It is important to Craig to teach other children how to get involved, so every summer, FTC runs leadership camps in Canada and the U.S. These are just a few of the group's accomplishments.

Nicaraguan children, with a message for Free the Children members who helped them

In 1996, Craig was awarded the Reebok Youth in Action Award—the same award that Iqbal Masih won just months before he was killed. As Craig received the award, he felt that Iqbal was watching over him. "Being recognized here is an honor," Craig told the crowd, "but the real heroes are the boys and girls who work in darkness, alone and forgotten. And by your actions, you can set them free!"

In the spring of 2001, Craig graduated from Mary Ward High School in Toronto, Canada. He plans to attend college, but first he is taking a year off to work full time, spreading Free the Children's message of compassion and taking action to change things for the better.

Life Lines

1982 Craig Kielburger is born in Toronto, Canada, December 17.

1995 On April 15, Craig reads an article in the *Toronto Star* about the death of Iqbal Masih, a Pakistani child-labor activist. In response, Craig founds Free the Children. That fall, he gives a speech at a convention of the Ontario Federation of Labor, and raises $150,000. In December, Craig travels to South Asia to witness child labor firsthand. He visits Bangladesh, India, Nepal, Thailand, and Pakistan.

1996 Craig is given the Reebok Youth in Action Award, the same award that Iqbal Masih won two years before.

1998 Craig publishes his autobiography, *Free the Children: A Young Man's Personal Crusade*. All money from the sale of the book is donated to Free the Children.

2001 Craig graduates from Mary Ward High School in Toronto.

Mother Teresa

born 1910 • died 1997

T he world has lost one of the giants of our time," said U.S. President Bill Clinton when Mother Teresa died. Born Agnes Gonxha Bojaxhiu, Mother Teresa became world famous for her work with the poorest of the world's poor. She won many awards and met regularly with world leaders, but throughout her life her focus remained on the destitute, the sick, and the dying.

A Yearning to Help

Agnes Gonxha Bojaxhiu was born August 26, 1910, in Skopje, which is now the capital of Macedonia. She grew up in a devout Roman Catholic family. As a teenager, she joined a church group devoted to helping the poor, and heard about missionaries working in India. She turned 18 determined to go to India and become a nun.

In 1928, Agnes joined the Sisters of Loreto, a group of nuns dedicated to teaching. In the Catholic Church, women who become nuns give up their birth names and take a new name. Agnes chose the name Teresa. She was sent to Calcutta, India, to teach in a school for girls. Later, she became the school's principal.

The poverty in Calcutta was—and still is—shocking. The poorest of the poor live on the streets, have no possessions, and often die young and alone of disease or starvation. At first, Sister Teresa rarely saw Calcutta's poor. The Sisters of Loreto was an "enclosed" order of nuns— they never went out. Then, in August, 1946, terrible violence broke out

Mother Teresa comforts a sick child in Calcutta, India.

between Hindus and Muslims in Calcutta. Thousands of people were killed in riots and the city completely shut down. Although there was a curfew, Sister Teresa went into the streets to find food for the girls in her school. On her way, she passed by one of the worst slums in the city.

A New Calling

A month later, on September 10, 1946, Sister Teresa again left the convent—this time, to attend a religious meeting. On the train ride there, she heard what she believed to be a call from God. "The message was quite clear," she said. "I was to leave the convent and work with the poor while living among them."

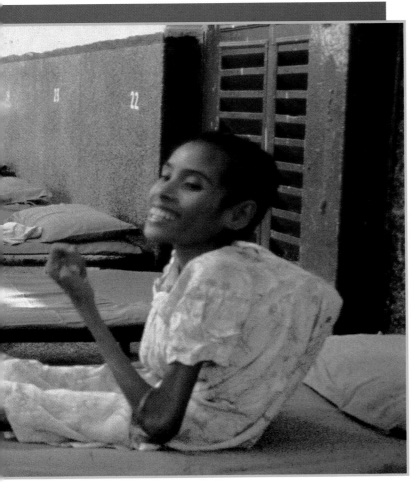

She received permission from the church, and soon found nuns to join her. She was now Mother Teresa and her new order of nuns was named the Missionaries of Charity.

One of Mother Teresa's first acts was to return to the slum near her former school and begin teaching the children there. At first, she had no supplies, so she began by scratching letters in the dusty ground. Then, in a building the city gave her, she set up the Home for the Dying. There, Calcutta's dying poor could come inside and, for once, be cared for. Mother Teresa and the other nuns walked through the home, talking to the patients, holding their hands, and easing their loneliness. "All we can give our people is a human death," she said. "We cannot let a child of God die like an animal in the gutter."

Mother Teresa's compassion and dedication continually attracted new followers, and she set up centers throughout the world. She became a media star in 1969, when a British television documentary brought her story to the West. When one of the filmmakers claimed that images

"I see God in every human being. When I wash the leper's wounds, I feel I am nursing the Lord himself."
—Mother Teresa

Mother Teresa being awarded the Nobel Peace Prize in Oslo, Norway, in 1979

Just One Example

It was 1982. Israel had invaded Beirut, Lebanon. Bombs were dropping and snipers' bullets flew through the air. Pope John Paul II sent Mother Teresa to Beirut to show his sympathy for the war's victims.

When Mother Teresa arrived there, she learned that 36 mentally ill children were trapped in a hospital on the front lines. Some of the children had starved to death.

Mother Teresa said that she was going to rescue the children. Officials said that it would be impossible without a cease-fire. At 4 p.m. on August 10, she prayed for a cease-fire. At 5 p.m., the bombs and bullets stopped. With a convoy from the International Red Cross, she drove to the hospital, comforted the terrified children, then took them to a Missionaries of Charity convent.

similar to halos appeared above Mother Teresa's head on the film, it attracted even more attention.

Whether Mother Teresa was a miracle worker or just extraordinarily caring, she never stopped searching for poor, abandoned people who needed her help. In 1979, she won the Nobel Peace Prize for her work. At her request, a celebratory dinner for her was canceled and the money was given to the poor. "We need to tell the poor that they are somebody to us," she said as she received the prize.

On Christmas Eve 1985, the Sisters of Charity came to the U.S. to open a center in New York City for dying AIDS patients. They called it Gift of Love. Mother Teresa said that helping people in the West was a special challenge. In the U.S., she said, "There is not only hunger for food. I see a big hunger for love. That is the greatest hunger—to be loved."

Mother Teresa died on September 5, 1997, at age 87. At that time, the Missionaries of Charity had more than 500 centers in 120 countries. In 1999, the Catholic Church began the lengthy process of declaring Mother Teresa a saint. To the many people she helped, she already is one.

Life Lines

1910 Agnes Gonxha Bojaxhiu is born in Skopje, now the capital of Macedonia, on August 26.

1928 Agnes joins the Sisters of Loreto, a group of nuns, and takes the name Teresa.

1931 Sister Teresa begins teaching at a school for girls in Calcutta, India.

1946 While on a train, Sister Teresa hears a call to live and work among the poor.

1950 The Pope, head of the Catholic Church, officially recognizes Mother Teresa's order, the Missionaries of Charity.

1979 Mother Teresa's work earns her the Nobel Peace Prize.

1997 Mother Teresa dies in Calcutta, India, on September 5.